I0571527

Three
QUESTIONS

Determining your

- IDENTITY
- DESTINY
- CALLING

Jim Wood

Copyright © 2010

by James P and Susan M Wood
All rights reserved.

ISBN: 0-9701855-7-X

2nd Printing

Unless otherwise noted Scripture Quotations
The Holy Bible, New International Version (NIV)
©1973, 1984 by International Bible Society
Used by permission of Zondervan Publishing House

Printed in the United States of America by:
Bethany Press International

Thank you!

Wears Valley Ranch and *Abiding in Christ* are a testimony to answered prayer. We depend solely on donations from the body of Christ. We incur no debt and accept no government funds. Gifts are tax-deductible. Find us at **WVR.org**

**P O Box 1600
Pigeon Forge, TN 37868
866-41ABIDE**

Listen to Jim on *Abiding in Christ*

- Weekdays on **SiriusXM** 131

- Download programs at WVR.org

- Jim's audio and video content is also available on Sermonaudio.com

Other Ministries include:

- Year round residential care for children from families in crisis
- St Andrew's School, fully accredited K-12, tutorial approach
- Recreation, including Equestrian, Adventure Recreation and Sports
- Master's level counseling
- Camp Arrowwood
- Retreats and Conferences
- College Mentoring Program
- Volunteer Program
- Resources - books, CD's and DVD's

WVR.org

CONTENTS

FOREWORD

Jim and I have been friends since our early teens. Before we finished high school, he already had a clear sense of God's call to do what he does today at Wears Valley Ranch.

This book springs from his desire to help people find their identity in Christ. Like a search light, Jim illuminates the key component to living the Christian life and that is to lean on the Holy Spirit within that has been given to each believer for wisdom, direction, and guidance through the land mines of our earthly dwelling.

5

Christ *in us* is what gives us power to live in the world without compromise. I hope you'll read *Three Questions*. You'll be glad you did.

Franklin Graham

President & CEO
Samaritan's Purse
Billy Graham Evangelistic Association

PREFACE

As I walked into a ballroom to speak at a weekend conference, I overheard a husband ask his wife, "How far in do you want to go?"

I chuckled and said to the man, "That's really the question, isn't it?"

This same question persists whether you're going into the river, a romance or a business venture. Likewise, whether you're contemplating involvement in a church or a new ministry, or whether it's simply a matter of following Jesus, sooner or later, you have to answer the question, "How far in do I want to go?"

We work hard to avoid some questions, because we don't want to face the answer. Other questions we wish that someone else would ask, because we feel foolish for not knowing the answer. Other times we ask questions and don't really listen to the answer.

You've probably been greeted with the question, "How are you doing?"

If you understand cultural norms, you know the proper and polite answer to this question is, "Fine."

Usually, when people say, "How ya' doin'," they really don't want to hear about how you're doing, especially if it involves anything negative.

We breeze through life asking some questions we don't want answered honestly.

This is why in most contexts we seldom make eye contact and walk by briskly, and when we do ask the question, we do not intend to listen for an answer. We breeze through life asking some questions we don't want answered honestly.

Some of us are "put off" when people give an honest answer. We learn early not to ask such questions of *those* people again. This is a sad reality, but isn't it true?

When I was a boy, my older siblings often teased my parents about their predictable answers to the question, "How are you doing?" They said Dad's tombstone would read, "I told you I was sick," and Mom's would read, "Really, I'm fine."

Although we didn't put it on Dad's tombstone, it turns out that it was somewhat true. Dad died at eighty-seven, only days after mother allowed him to stop taking his "daily constitutional" walk. Mom died at ninety-nine and the last time we asked her the question, she gave the expected response, "I'm fine."

When I was a child, there were certain questions I loved. I particularly liked it when one of my parents asked, "What would you like to do today?" I loved that question, though I think I only heard it maybe two or three times in childhood.

On my birthday Mom would ask, "What would you like for dinner?" I loved that question. I love to eat. I've always had opinions on the subjects of breakfast, lunch and supper. Therefore, I always had a ready answer to that question.

I also loved it when I was eating at someone else's house and the hostess asked, "Would you like some more?"

Those were wonderful questions, but there were other questions I didn't like.

You may remember hearing these questions from your childhood. They were asked rhetorically, so though no answer was expected or allowed, these questions struck fear in the heart:

Who do you think you are? Where do you think you're going? What do you think you're doing?

I hated those questions, because I knew the question meant that I was already in trouble. No answer would suffice. Any answer my childish mind might concoct would most certainly be the wrong answer.

As I got older, I learned that these questions are brilliant. Your own answers to these questions may not necessarily be true, but I can guarantee you this:

What you believe about who you are has an enormous impact on everything else in your life.

What you believe about who you are has an enormous impact on everything else in your life. What you believe about yourself affects all of your relationships. It affects the most important relationship in your life — your relationship with God.

Because these three questions are essential, I want to look at each one and find the answers in God's Word, the Bible.

13

Who do you think you are?

Perhaps you've heard of the self-made man who worshipped his creator.

Many folks don't have a right understanding of who they are. They don't understand the truth and are deluded about who they are.

15

Three QUESTIONS

Some of the most selfish people I've dealt with have told me with utter sincerity and apparent psychosis, "I think my real problem is I just care about others too much."

I think to myself in that moment, "How can a person who is so totally self-absorbed sit there and say, 'I need to think more of myself'?"

I try to explain to them that they have it backwards. We don't know ourselves as well as we should.

 Who do you think you are?

You may or may not have a biblical view of your identity, but what you believe about who you are has a profound impact on the answer to question number two:

 Where do you think you're going?

When I was growing up, I used to try to find ways to talk with my friends about the gospel. I sometimes asked, "What do you plan to be doing five years from now?"

Often the answer would be, "College, I guess."

My response, "That's great. What do you plan to do after college?"

"I don't know."

"What would you like to do?"

Three QUESTIONS

"I don't know. I'd like to own my own business, I think."

"Well, that's great. Then, what do you want to do?"

"I'd like to probably get married."

"Then what?"

"I want to make a lot of money and be able to retire early."

"If you made a lot of money and could retire early, then what would you like to do?"

"I don't know. Go fishing, I guess."

"That's great. Then, what do you plan to do?"

Who do you think you are?

Eventually we'd get to the real point and they'd finally say, "I guess I'll die."

"Right, and then what are you going to do?"

Most people live their lives with virtually no clue about where they will spend eternity.

Often, these kinds of questions have led to discussions in which I have had the honor to lead people to Christ. I love pointing out to people that most of us have an idea of what we'd like to do for the next seventy years or so, but it seems like most people live their lives with virtually no clue about where they will spend eternity.

Three QUESTIONS

Whether you have genes like mine that might enable you to live to a hundred years old or longer, or whether you have genes that will take you out in your sixties or seventies, however much time you hope to have here on earth, that time is still finite, and, ultimately, it is not the most important issue.

What happens after you die is forever. Planning for the next thirty or forty years is a good idea. Planning for eternity is essential. What you believe about who you are has a profound impact on what you believe about where you're going. Only if we live in light of eternity can we have the kind of life we should have in the here and now.

Who do you think you are?

Answering the questions: "Who do you think you are?" and "Where do you think you're going?" shapes your answer to the third question: "What do you think you're doing?"

Think for a moment:

 Who do you think you are?

If someone had asked you this question last night, how would you have answered? How do you define yourself?

A lot of us introduce ourselves in terms of what we do for a living: "I'm Jim Wood. I'm the Executive Director of a children's home."

The problem with defining myself in terms of a job is that I may outlive my job. Then, who am I? Defining ourselves in terms of our work tends to lead to a bunch of "has-beens."

I spend a fair amount of time with precious Christians in places that have an elderly median age. I preach in some churches where the average age is over seventy-five. These aren't usually dying churches; rather, they are churches located in retirement communities. Some of the people still live vibrant lives, but often when I talk with them, they say things like:

"I used to be an attorney."

"I used to be in sales."

"I used to be a banker."

Who do you think you are?

"This is my husband, Fred. He was a doctor."

I think to myself, "How sad to be a 'was' already. How sad it is to define yourself in terms of what you used to do."

There are churches full of "has-beens."

Some of us find new ways to define ourselves, "We're the grandparents of thirteen."

Defining ourselves in terms of relationships has the potential of lasting longer than defining ourselves in terms of a career. You can even keep updating your resume as babies are born. The problem is that even these earthly relationships begin to lose their power to give us the kind of identity God wants us to have.

Only one relationship should define who we are - our relationship with God in Jesus Christ.

Only one relationship should define who we are - our relationship with God in Jesus Christ. If we get this relationship right, it changes everything.

However, I want to submit to you that the Scriptures are very, very clear about the dangers of presuming upon a relationship with God that you don't have.

Many people believe, "Well, we're all God's children."

Who do you think you are?

I want to offer some particularly neglected words of Jesus spoken to those who refused to recognize **who he is**:

...You belong to your father, the devil, and you want to carry out your father's desire. He was a murderer from the beginning, not holding to the truth, for there is no truth in him. When he lies, he speaks his native language, for he is a liar and the father of lies.[1]

When I was child, we had a promise box on the kitchen table full of little cards with isolated "feel good" verses to make us happy. We could pull one out each morning as we headed off to school or work. In our current more affluent age people put these "happy thoughts" on ministry calendars. This verse was not in the promise boxes or on the ministry calendars designed to uplift us in our walk with God.

You belong to your father the devil, and you want to carry out your father's desire.

Some folks recoil when they hear such things: "That's not nice. I don't like that verse."

Can you imagine if you flipped your calendar to the next month and John 8:44 stared you in the face? This sounds more like a sadistic fortune cookie, doesn't it?

You belong to your father, the devil.

"Only a 'sicko' would say something like that."

26

Who do you think you are?

Jesus said it himself. *Jesus* said it. He didn't say it to everybody. He said it to people who hated him. Nevertheless, he did say it.

Intellectual assent is not Christian faith.

In the end, what defines you is your relationship with Jesus Christ. If your relationship with Jesus Christ is like that of the devil — "I will not submit to Christ; I do not want to bow to him" — you are in peril.

Intellectual assent is not Christian faith: *You believe that there is one God. Good! Even the demons believe that — and shudder.*[2]

Three QUESTIONS

God promises, *'As surely as I live,'* says the Lord, *'every knee will bow before me; every tongue will confess to God.'*3

Even those hostile to him now will bow before him, because Jesus Christ is Lord. He's not running for office. He is Lord.

Because Jesus is Lord, those who bow now, who honor him now, who receive forgiveness by grace through faith now, will have a relationship with him that lasts forever.

Again, God warns us not to take this relationship for granted. Don't presume upon God's grace:

*Make your calling and election sure.*4

Does Jesus know you? *Many will say to me on that day, 'Lord, Lord, did we not prophesy in your name, and in your name drive out demons and perform many miracles?'*

I will tell them plainly, 'I never knew you. Away from me, you evildoers!'[5]

This is sobering. This is serious. This is scary.

The apostle Paul warns the Corinthians: *Do you not know that the wicked will not inherit the kingdom of God? Do not be deceived: Neither the sexually immoral nor idolaters nor adulterers nor male prostitutes nor homosexual offenders nor thieves nor the greedy nor drunkards nor slanderers nor swindlers will inherit the kingdom of God. And that is what some of you were. But you were washed, you were sanctified, you were justified in the name of the Lord Jesus Christ and by the Spirit of our God.[6]*

We don't hear this preached much today, because it's not a happy thought. However, we need to speak the Truth. We need to preach the whole counsel of God.

1 John 5:13 is a wonderful place to go for assurance: *I write these things to you who believe in the name of the Son of God so that you may know that you have eternal life.*

When you read 1 John 5 in its full context, depending on who you think you are, this passage is either reassuring or alarming.

The verses, which precede verse 13, give us vital signs: *...This is how we know that*

Who do you think you are?

we love the children of God: by loving God and carrying out his commands. This is love for God: to obey his commands. ...[7]

If you manifest God's transforming grace, you can know God has changed you. However, if you are still trying to defend yourself and pursue your own goals, be warned that you are still unregenerate and living in your sins.

When God saves us, he changes us from the inside out. If this is true of you, John writes, you have evidence of Christ's Spirit living in you. If you are still clinging to your sin and refusing to forgive others, then you are a liar when you say you are God's child.[8]

At the conclusion of all these proofs, John writes: *I write these things to you who believe in the name of the Son of God so that you may know that you have eternal life.*[9]

John doesn't write so that anyone who reads this verse will know that they have eternal life, but so that those who recognize God's grace, whose trust is in him, will know that they have eternal life.

Let me summarize: ... *if we claim to be without sin, we deceive ourselves and the truth is not in us. If we confess our sins, he is faithful and just and will forgive us our sins and purify us from all unrighteousness.*[10]

What determines who we are, finally, is whether we are trusting in Jesus or in ourselves. The apostle Paul warned the Galatians that if they submitted themselves to circumcision, they were cut off from Christ.[11]

Either you are IN CHRIST or you are still dead in your sins.

You can't trust in God's grace alone and, at the same time, try to earn your salvation. You can't have it both ways.

Either you are IN CHRIST or you are still dead in your sins.[12]

He who believes in the Son has eternal life; but he who does not obey the Son ['obey' is the same word as 'trust' in the Greek] will not see life, but the wrath of God abides on him. [13]

I want to ask you a question:

Three QUESTIONS

 Who do you think you are?

Those who are in Christ should be encouraged.

Be warned, though. Even if you do not know the Lord, the devil will try to make you feel good about yourself.

If you do know the Lord, the devil will work very hard to make you feel you are worthless, a total failure, and that God couldn't possibly love you.

The devil will bombard your mind with the opposite of the Truth. He is a liar. This is why we need to keep going back to God's Word and see what God says.

What does God say about who I am?

Who do you think you are?

In 1 John 3:1-3 Christians read: *How great is the love the Father has lavished on us, that we should be called children of God! And that is what we are! The reason the world does not know us is that it did not know him. Dear friends, now we are children of God, and what we will be has not yet been made known. But we know that when he appears we shall be like him, for we shall see him as he is. Everyone who has this hope in him purifies himself, just as he is pure.*

John calls us the children of God. Do you know why? That is what we are.

So, ...

 *Who do you think **you** are?*

Three QUESTIONS

I am a child of God, and this is very encouraging to me:

But you are a chosen people, a royal priesthood, a holy nation, a people belonging to God, that you may declare the praises of him who called you out of darkness into his wonderful light.[14]

A child at the Ranch wore a T-shirt that read *I am an alien* based on the following verses:

Dear friends, I urge you, as aliens and strangers in the world, to abstain from sinful desires, which war against your soul. Live such good lives among the pagans that, though they accuse you of doing wrong, they may see your good deeds and glorify God on the day he visits us.[15]

Who do you think you are?

It's true. If you are a Christian, you're an alien and stranger in this world. You may not like being an alien, but if you are a follower of Jesus Christ that is exactly what you are.

On the other hand, if you are in love with this world, you do not love God. *The man who **loves** his life will lose it, while the man who hates his life in this **world** will keep it for eternal life.*[16]

Do not love the world or anything in the world. If anyone loves the world, the love of the Father is not in him.[17]

Does this describe you?

If you belonged to the world, it would love you as its own. As it is, you do not belong to the world, but I have chosen you out of the world. That is why the world hates you.[18]

Three QUESTIONS

Do not conform any longer to the pattern of this world, but be transformed by the renewing of your mind. Then you will be able to test and approve what God's will is — his good, pleasing and perfect will.[19]

If you're a follower of Jesus Christ, you need to realize that the reason you don't "fit in" is because you're an alien, a stranger in this world.

Who do I think I am? I am a child of God. I am a priest. I am holy.

"Holy? Is that a good thing? Isn't it an insult to be called holier than thou?"

If you are a follower of Christ, you are holier than those who don't follow him. Genuine followers are holy, set apart.

Who do you think you are?

They do not conform to this world. They obey their Lord, Jesus Christ.[20]

Have you ever heard someone say, "Well, I don't pretend to be a saint?"

I don't pretend to be a saint either. I *am* one.

I don't pretend to be a man. I *am* one.

I don't pretend to be married. I *am* married.

I *am* a saint.

I *am* holy.

So are you, if you are a follower of Jesus Christ. You shouldn't pretend anything, but if you're a follower of Jesus, you *are* a saint.

Three QUESTIONS

"I thought you had to die and work miracles from the grave to be a saint."

Nope, that's not in the Scriptures. What does the book say? What does God tell us in his Word?

Among other things, God's children are told that we are saints. We are holy, set apart. We belong to God in Christ Jesus. He purchased us. Our bodies are the temple of the Holy Spirit. We, his children, are God's building. We are living stones being fitted together to provide a beautiful habitation for a Holy God. We, the church, are the bride of Christ.[21]

Do you ever feel like, "God couldn't possibly love me"?

Who do you think you are?

Christian, he loves you. He really, really loves you, even though you don't deserve his love. He loves you anyway.

Because God loves me, I can handle the rejection of others.

I am amazed that God loves me, and God is the only one who knows everything about me. He knows me better than my mama knows me. He knows me better than I know myself. He knows everything about me; yet, he loves me.

Because God loves me, I can handle the rejection of others. If God accepts me in Christ Jesus, then I am truly accepted. God truly knows me, and God truly loves me.

Three QUESTIONS

I [Jesus] am the vine; you are the branches.[22]

We are his [God's] people, the sheep of his pasture.[23]

You are a holy person, if you belong to Jesus. God has gifted you. You have something to contribute to others.

In 1 Corinthians 12:15-26, Paul says:

If the foot should say, 'Because I am not a hand, I do not belong to the body,' it would not for that reason cease to be part of the body. And if the ear should say, 'Because I am not an eye, I do not belong to the body,' it would not for that reason cease to be part of the body. If the whole body were an eye, where would the sense of hearing be? If the whole body were an ear, where would the sense of smell be? But in fact God has arranged the parts in the body, every one of them, just as he wanted them to be. If they were all one part, where would the body be? As it is, there are many parts, but one body.

The eye cannot say to the hand, 'I don't need you!' And the head cannot say to the feet, 'I don't need you!' On the contrary, those parts of the body that seem to be weaker are indispensable, and the parts that we think are less honorable we treat with special honor. And the parts that are unpresentable are treated with special modesty, while our presentable parts need no special treatment. But God has combined the members of the body and has given greater honor to the parts that lacked it, so that there should be no division in the body, but that its parts should have equal concern for each other. If one part suffers, every part suffers with it; if one part is honored, every part rejoices with it.

Your self-image influences how you relate to others, but it doesn't negate the fact that if you're a child of God, you have value. You have something to bring to the table. God has made you his own, and through his Spirit, he has gifted you to be a blessing to other people. Do not embrace the devil's lie that you have nothing to contribute.

I have a brother-in-law whose younger sister is developmentally disabled. Because of her learning difficulties, she had real trouble reading as a young student. Her oldest brother is a powerful evangelist. Her second oldest brother is a surgeon. Her third oldest brother is an attorney.

My evangelist brother-in-law told me how impressed he is with the wisdom God has given his sister. As a student, she would approach teachers and other staff members in her school with a gospel tract and ask, "Would you read this to me?"

She wanted to witness to people at her school, but she didn't know how. Finally, she came up with an original idea. I think the Holy Spirit helped her. She knew that those willing to read the tract aloud to her would be exposed to the gospel of Jesus Christ.

With a simple question, "Would you read this to me?" she had the opportunity to share the gospel with more people than many intellectually gifted people who claim a relationship with Christ. She shared God's love. She shared his message.

Three QUESTIONS

You have a gift. I don't care what your background is or how many IQ points you do or do not have; God has gifted you to bless others beyond anything you might imagine. You are gifted and you have a place in the body of Christ. Jesus says to His followers:

You are the salt of the earth. ... You are the light of the world.[24]

Jesus doesn't ask, "How many of you would be willing to be salt?"

Jesus informs his followers, "You are the salt."

Jesus doesn't ask, "How many of you would be willing to be light?"

Jesus tells us, "You are the light."

Who do you think you are?

Are you going to decay in your surroundings or are you going to be salty?

Are you going to be salty salt? Are you going to be a light that shines? Are you going to hide your light under a bushel or are you going to shine and expose the deeds of darkness? Are you going to decay in your surroundings or are you going to be salty?

God tells us who we are in his Word; we can't begin to unpack it all. Ask God to show you who you are in the light of his Word. Ask him to help you understand from Scripture what he says about you so that you stop believing garbage and lies that the world would use to try to distort God's image in you.

Three QUESTIONS

You are created in the image and likeness of God. Sin marred that image, but because of Jesus Christ, you are now being transformed from the inside out by the renewing of your mind as God's word changes the way you view everything, including who you think you are. You are an ambassador for Jesus Christ.[25]

The Vatican repeatedly turned down President Obama's appointments for US ambassador to the Vatican. He kept trying to send pro-choice, pro-abortion advocates. In response to Obama's appointment of Caroline Kennedy, the Vatican said, "No, we will not receive her as US ambassador." Her family connections did not negate her stances on essential questions of morality.

Who do you think you are?

Did you know that while governments negotiate over who does and does not get to be an ambassador, if you are a follower of Jesus Christ, you *are* an ambassador. When you go to work, you don't just represent your family or your community, you represent Jesus Christ. You *are* an ambassador. Wherever you live, wherever you work, whatever you do, you are a representative of God's government, God's kingdom. You are an ambassador for him.

An ambassador must represent his ruler while being sensitive to the culture where he is sent. The ambassador must realize at all times that what he does reflects on the one he represents. So, if you're going to be an ambassador for Jesus Christ, that changes how you conduct yourself, doesn't it? You can't just do what comes naturally.

The students at the Ranch love the story I tell about an event in the grocery store in my younger years. When I was in seminary in New England, a woman was very rude to me. She intentionally cut in front of me in the line where I was standing and waiting my turn, and then she spun around and glared at me. She acted victorious in her coup to overtake me in the line. She was gloating; she was glaring. She made it seem that I had done something offensive.

In that moment the impulse that arose in me was a desire to bark at her. She had a bulldog look. When she looked at me in that hateful way, I wanted to respond with a deep guttural, menacing bark.

I couldn't do it, because I am an ambassador. If the woman had had a heart attack in response to my barking, this seminary student would have had a hard time explaining my behavior.

How would I explain the barking? Maybe it was her physiognomy. The way she presented herself brought out the animal in me.

Because I am an ambassador of Jesus Christ, a child of God, a servant of the Most High, I can't just do what comes naturally. I can't just follow my impulses. It changes everything if you know who you are.

Three QUESTIONS

 Who do you think you are?

I want to encourage those of you who have given your lives to Jesus to get before God, look into his Word and see what he says about you. Realize that you are a joint heir with Christ. You are destined for great things. In light of who you are, you have marvelous things in store.

I hope you will continually look into God's Word and be reminded of who you are. Many folks are mistaken about who they are. Their view of themselves is not biblical but shaped by the culture, and based on things they heard repeatedly growing up.

Who do you think you are?

Obviously, we deal with this issue all the time at Wears Valley Ranch as we work with children who have been abused, not only physically and sexually, but also emotionally. They've been told:

"You'll never amount to anything."

"You're no good."

"You're stupid."

"You can't learn."

Often, the things that shape our sense of identity are diabolical. They are the lies of the Enemy. It is vital that we get our sense of identity from what God says about who we are in Christ, if indeed we are in Christ.

Three QUESTIONS

Have you come to the point where you recognize your sin and agree with God that you deserve his wrath and need a Savior?

Before you go further, you need to settle the question of your identity. Have you come to the point in your own life where you recognize your sin and agree with God that you deserve his wrath and need a Savior? Have you trusted Jesus as the One who took your punishment and paid for your sin on the cross? Have you asked him to forgive you and take control of your life? Until you reach the end of yourself and ask him to give you a new life, you will not know the joy and peace that go beyond circumstances and feelings. I hope you'll settle it now! You may want to pray something like this:

Dear God,
I know I have sinned, and there is nothing I can do to earn your love. I don't deserve to go to heaven. I deserve hell. But, I believe the Bible is true. Thank you for loving me. Thank you for sending Jesus to die on the cross to pay for my sins. Please, take control of my life. Remove my guilt. I am trusting you to forgive me and take me to heaven when I die. Please, fill me with your Holy Spirit and change me from the inside out. I want to become everything you want me to be and do what you want me to do.

Where do you think you're going?

There are three principle views that seem to dominate the landscape with regard to this question. The first view growing in popularity, especially among young people today, is the view of an atheist, a secularist, a materialist. A view that says, "This life is all there is. You only go around once, you die, and then you turn back to dirt."

Not only will there be no dogs and cats in heaven in the view of these people, there is no heaven. This life is all there is. We are pieces of highly evolved slime, and when our time is up, we go back into the ground and turn into mulch. That's it. There is no future. There is no life beyond the grave.

Many people believe this, because it's a convenient view, particularly when they're young. If there is no God and there is no future beyond the grave,

If there is no resurrection, we might as well "eat and drink, for tomorrow we die."

then I can do whatever I please. In fact, the Bible refers to this line of thinking. The apostle Paul tells the Corinthians that if there is no resurrection, we might as well "eat and drink, for tomorrow we die."

This is not a new idea. It is regaining some popularity in our culture, but it is a very old view. I doubt that many who would read this book hold this view, but you need to be aware that many people do hold this view.

The apostle Paul says: *If only for this life we have hope in Christ, we are to be pitied more than all men.* [26]

Three QUESTIONS

Real Christianity involves living a transformed life, and if the life of a Christian were only for this temporal life, it is a very foolish way to live. The Christian life is a life of intentional self-sacrifice. We are commanded to take up our cross daily. We are called to die to our own desires and listen for the voice of the Holy Spirit. We are called to obey even when it might cost us everything. Christians live in light of eternity. Where we believe we're going has a profound impact on whether or not we go where we are called to go now.

There is a second view that is more popular than you might imagine. It is belief in reincarnation. It's not just for "wing nuts" like Shirley MacLaine and other aging "New Agers," who once upon a time were young hippies. There really are many other folks in the world that we need to be aware of even as we live in a somewhat insular community.

Over sixteen percent of the world population is from India and that number is rapidly climbing. Many of these folks, plus others around the world, are Hindu. Even people who don't claim to be Hindu — they might just claim to be talk show hosts — are imbibing this belief in reincarnation. They really believe they are in a continuous process of being recycled. They want to do the right thing so they can come back as something better in the next life.

Three QUESTIONS

It is interesting to me that almost all of them believe they used to be a princess or a duchess. Nobody used to be a maid. Nobody used to be a galley boy. They were, instead, an admiral or a pirate. It's very sad. It's embarrassing: "I know I may not have amounted to much in this life, but in my last life, if you could have known me, then I was somebody. I was a hot ticket. I was the original Casanova."

There is a desire to tap into something bigger, but obviously an enormous resistance to getting to know God. The belief in reincarnation is a convenient way to avoid the reality: *...man is destined to die once, and after that to face judgment.*[27]

Where do you think you're going?

Man is destined to die once, and after that to face judgment.

The biblical view is that all of us, after we die, are going to have to give an account before God. Every single person on the planet is going to spend eternity either in heaven or in hell. There is no limbo. There is no purgatory — no neutral place for those who didn't get their act together in time. There's not someplace else to go and work off your sins and impurities.

"What can wash away my sin? Nothing but the blood of Jesus."[28]

Every single person on the planet is going to spend forever somewhere. The

Three QUESTIONS

Bible tells us there are two options: Heaven or hell. Going to heaven is not based on "good Karma." It is not based on the Muslim view of doing more good than bad. It's based on one thing alone: your relationship with Jesus Christ.

This is why the thief on the cross could be promised: *"Today you will be with me in paradise."*[29]

Even though he had made a mess of his life, as he hung there dying, he clearly confessed his faith in Jesus as Savior and Lord. He didn't say, "Hey, I know I got in trouble with the law here at the end of my life, but I want you to know, Jesus, I really was a good person." The thief simply asked for mercy, and Jesus

Where do you think you're going?

said, *"Today you will be with me in paradise."*

Among those who would agree that we're going to be in either heaven or hell are many people who, according to Jesus, will be very surprised that they're going to hell. I referenced Matthew 7 previously. Jesus said:

Many will say to me on that day, 'Lord, Lord, did we not prophesy in your name, and in your name drive out demons and perform many miracles?' Then I will tell them plainly, 'I never knew you. Away from me, you evildoers!'[30]

If you encountered someone who was able to prophesy (that is, speak forth the word of God) and they were able to perform miracles and cast out demons, wouldn't you say, "That person is definitely going to heaven. I'm not sure about myself sometimes, because I haven't done all the things I know I should do, but that guy is going to heaven."

Jesus says, "No, there will be bunches of people like that to whom I will say, '*I never knew you. Away from me, you evildoers!*'[31]

"I don't know, Pastor, you're making me nervous. I was doing well up until now. You always have a knack for making me feel worse. Is that your ministry?"

I sometimes tell people, "Barnabas was the son of encouragement. I am Barnacle, the son of discouragement." My job is to make you feel bad.

Where do you think you're going?

Dr. Gerstner, a famous preacher of a previous generation, was approached at the door after he had preached—probably on the exceeding sinfulness of sin—by a woman who said, "Dr. Gerstner, you made me feel about this big," holding her thumb and forefinger about half an inch apart.

He looked at her and said in his extremely deep and gravelly voice, "Madam, that is too big."

Folks, none of us deserve to go to heaven. If you've had any training in *Evangelism Explosion* or another similar program designed to teach you to share your faith, you know the diagnostic questions:

Three QUESTIONS

"Have you come to the place in your spiritual life that you know for certain you have eternal life?"

Some people say, "No, I don't know. I'd like to go to heaven, but I'm not sure."

Some people say, "Yes, I know I'm going to heaven."

The second diagnostic question is: "If, God forbid, you were to die right now, and suddenly you had to stand before God and God were to ask you, 'Why should I let you into my heaven,' what would your answer be?"

At this point, you find out where a person's confidence is. I have asked this question of thousands of people, and the answers are just amazing. The late D.

Where do you think you're going?

James Kennedy used to say that people don't like canned evangelism, but if you go ahead and ask the questions, you'll find that most people give you canned answers. Person after person will tell you the same thing:

"Well, I've tried to live a good life. I know I've messed up sometimes, but I've done the best I know how."

My favorite answer, and I've heard it from at least half the people I've asked, is that they've never killed anybody. They say this as if they're expecting me to be really impressed. I want to say to my wife, "Honey, quick, go get the camera. This person has never killed anyone."

Three QUESTIONS

They seem convinced that if not killing anyone doesn't qualify them for heaven, they don't know what will. That's the problem: They don't know what will. They think God grades on the curve.

Fritz Ridenour in his book, *How to be a Christian without being Religious*—a wonderful study of the book of Romans—points out that God doesn't grade on the curve. You and I don't get into heaven based on a comparison to Osama bin Laden or Adolf Hitler or Joseph Stalin or Pol Pot or some other notorious sinner.

All of us have sinned and fall short of the glory of God. The wages of sin is death.[32]

Then, how can a person be saved?

Where do you think you're going?

It's only through Jesus Christ. It's only through his sacrifice on the cross. He died on the cross to pay for our sins. He rose from the dead as conqueror over death and hell. He is our only hope. Our only hope! If you have hope in anything else, you're not on your way to heaven.

"What about those people in Matthew 7? They prophesied and cast out demons."

Yes, they did. Precisely. If you look at what they say when they stand before the judgment, they want to talk about what they did: "Lord, Lord, didn't we do this? Didn't we do that? We did this. Look at what we did. Surely, we get in. We called you our Lord. We prophesied in your name. We cast out demons. God, you used me."

Three QUESTIONS

God can use a donkey. He can.

"That's not true. Donkeys can't talk."

They can if God wants them to talk.

"Have you been watching Shrek?"

No, I've been reading my Bible. Balaam was the seer who couldn't see the angel who was about to kill him. God gave Balaam's donkey the gift of speech, so that the donkey said to Balaam: *What have I done to you to make you beat me these three times?*[33]

Now get this: Balaam actually answered. I would love to have been there. First, you get the amazing spectacle of the donkey talking to the prophet, but then, you get the prophet talking back to the donkey.

Where do you think you're going?

The difference between magic and miracles is who's in charge.

God can speak through a donkey. God can speak through a bush. God can speak through a person who is a fraud. The difference between magic and miracles is who's in charge, who's calling the shots.

Back in the 1970's, while making a movie about the fact that he wasn't really a Christian, Marjoe Gortner actually led some people to a saving faith in Christ. He didn't really believe the gospel and later made it clear that he was just a charlatan duping a bunch of ignorant people. I know this, because I know some of the people he led to Christ who were horrified when they found out that he was a fraud.

The apostle Paul describes this precise scenario in his letter to the Philippians. There are people who preach out of false motives, but the gospel is still true. If I preach the gospel, there will be people who get saved, but that won't save me. If I think I'm a Christian because God is able to use me, I have another thing coming. An intellectual faith in Jesus that says, "I believe these propositions are true," isn't the same thing as a trust relationship with Jesus that says, "You are my Lord. Lord, you're in charge; I want to do your will."

Are you getting your marching orders from God or are you trying to manipulate God to get God to do your thing? This is what salvation comes down to, and this is where each of us has to be very careful.

We don't want to buy into a vending machine approach to God, but rather we say: "Okay, God, I'm so sorry. I want to be obedient to your leading. I want to do what you say. I want to walk in your ways. I belong to you. Give the marching orders, and I'll obey."

We are not saved by what we do; Jesus saves us.

We are not saved by what we do; Jesus saves us. Jesus is our Lord and we obey him.

Three QUESTIONS

"There has to be something I bring to the table."

Yes, there is. You bring your sin. You bring your need. You and I were dead in trespasses and sin. The Bible doesn't say we had a little limp: "Yeah, I sinned and shot myself in the foot. It was really embarrassing."

No, we were dead, dead in trespasses and sins, and God made us alive in Christ Jesus. Salvation is his work.

"Yeah, but you do have to believe, right?"

Of course you do. Yet, he is *the author and perfecter of our faith.*[34]

"But, you have to repent, right?"

Where do you think you're going?

Yes, and *God's kindness leads you toward repentance.*[35]

John Newton got it right: "Amazing grace, how sweet the sound that saved a wretch like me. ... 'Twas grace that taught my heart to fear and grace my fears relieved." You see, it's God's doing.

In Titus we read:

At one time we too were foolish, disobedient, deceived and enslaved by all kinds of passions and pleasures. We lived in malice and envy, being hated and hating one another. But when the kindness and love of God our Savior appeared, he saved us, not because of righteous things we had done, but because of his mercy. He saved us through the washing of rebirth and renewal by the Holy Spirit, whom he poured out on us

*generously through Jesus Christ our Savior,
so that, having been justified by his grace,
we might become heirs having the hope of
eternal life.*[36]

Do you hear this? More importantly, do
you believe it? He says it twice in verse
5: "He saved us..." Internalize this. Say it
aloud: "He saved me. I don't deserve it,
but he saved me."

This is absolutely crucial, because it is at
the heart of the problem in Galatia. Paul
writes to the Galatians and rebukes
them harshly, not because they had
started worshipping idols or engaging
in all kinds of sexual immorality, but
because they were trying to do
something in order to make themselves
okay with God.

Where do you think you're going?

Unfortunately, I tend to like people who behave like the Galatians. I think they're really conscientious. I think they have a wonderful attitude.

Here's a group of Gentile men who hear that if you really want to be a Christian, you need to get circumcised. They are told, "God can't accept you as one of his children unless you are circumcised."

These Gentile Galatians respond, "I didn't know that. Nobody told me. If I had known, I would have already done it. Where do I sign up? And by the way, what is circumcision anyway?"

When Paul writes to them, he doesn't say, "Guys, you don't have to do this. It's not necessary. I mean, it's really sweet of you and everything, but ..."

Three QUESTIONS

Instead, the apostle Paul says, "You foolish Galatians. Who has bewitched you? You started out well. You trusted in Christ. You believed the gospel. Now, you're totally off course. "

Remember, these Galatians are very nice people who want to do the right thing. Instead of commending them, Paul says, "You're way out of line here." This must have seemed a shocking response from Paul.

They ask, "You're saying I shouldn't be circumcised?"

Paul has to explain, "Circumcision doesn't count for anything. But, in light of the significance that you are attaching to circumcision, I'm telling you the truth, if you get circumcised, you're cut off, severed from Christ."

That's a dreadful thought. The Gentile Galatians had to make a choice about who and what they believe.

They thought they had heard from reliable Christian teachers that they must be circumcised, and now Paul, the man who led them to faith in Christ, is saying they must not get circumcised. What a tough situation.

Paul desperately wants the Galatians to understand that the reason they must not be circumcised is not because circumcision is bad. Paul was circumcised. The reason is because if you think there is anything you can do to make yourself okay with God, you're

81

Three QUESTIONS

You can't get saved by something you do. **Only Jesus can save you.**

still lost. You can't get saved by something you do. Only Jesus can save you.

As a pastor, I cannot count the number of folks who have come to me over the years for counsel explaining to me, "I just want to make sure I've done the right thing. I prayed the prayer, and I got baptized, but I'm not sure I really understood it at the time. I did believe, but I'm not sure that I believed enough. I want to be sure that I said the right thing."

Do you know the problem with this? These people still think their salvation is dependent on something they do. They want to be sure that they prayed the prayer the right way. They want to be sure that they got baptized the right way and that the preacher used the right words as he baptized them. They want to be sure that they understood enough. Jesus said:

I praise you, Father, Lord of heaven and earth, because you have hidden these things from the wise and learned and revealed them to little children. Yes, Father, for this was your good pleasure.[37]

Some of the most clearly regenerate saints I've had the privilege to baptize had Down's syndrome and other kinds of mental retardation. Jesus never said, "You must become like a PhD in order to inherit the kingdom of God." He said, "You must become like a child."[38]

Salvation is not about how deep your theology is.

*It's about **who** you trust.*

Salvation is not about how deep your theology is. It's about who you trust. If you think you know enough, you're wrong. You'll never know enough.

"I used to be a bad guy. I used to do a lot of bad stuff. Now, I've turned over a new leaf, and I'm really learning how to do the right thing, putting one foot in front of the other, one day at a time. I'm making it."

"No, you've missed the point."

Where do you think you're going?

"But, I've cleaned up my act, man. I have cleaned up my act."

"If that's your attitude, you're still going to hell."

Years ago as I was visiting in the gym with a group of college students, one of the young women told me she couldn't become a Christian because she had a bad habit that would prevent her from becoming a Christian.

I asked, "What's the habit?"

She said, "My friends can tell you," and she went outside.

I turned to her friends and said, "Okay, she said it's alright to tell me. So, what's her habit?"

Three QUESTIONS

One of her friends spoke up and said, "Marijuana."

I ran out of the gym and caught up with the young woman and said, "Your friend said your habit is marijuana."

She responded, "That's right."

I said, "Let me share the gospel with you."

It's not anything we do; it's what Jesus did.

I talked to her about the fact that God is real, the gospel is true and that Jesus Christ died on the cross to pay for our sins. It's not anything we do; it's what Jesus did. Your trust needs to be in him.

Where do you think you're going?

This young woman finally came to the point where she believed. Of course, I was praying for God to open her eyes, open her heart.

God is the one who must take the blinders off our eyes. In Acts 16 we read of how Lydia's heart was opened. God is the one who must take the heart of stone and give us a heart of flesh. That's God's work.

Finally, the young woman said, "I'm ready to receive Christ, but before I do," she reached inside her bra and pulled out a packet of marijuana cigarettes, "I need to get rid of these."

Given this young woman's situation, I said to her, "No, you need to put those back."

Three QUESTIONS

"What?"

"Put those back. If you think you can clean up your act so that Jesus will save you, you're not going to be saved. Put them back."

She put the marijuana back in her bra and said, "Okay, now what?"

I told her, "Now we're going to talk to Jesus."

We prayed together. She confessed the fact that she was a sinner and that she deserved to go to hell. She believed that God loved her enough to send Jesus to die on the cross to pay for her sins. Even though she didn't deserve it, she wanted to receive the gift of eternal life right then and there.

Where do you think you're going?

She passed from death to life, *right then and there.* After we finished praying and she thanked God for saving her, I asked, "Now that you're a follower of Jesus Christ, what do you want to do with that stuff?"

She said, "I want to get rid of it."

I said, "Good for you."

We threw it away in a place where someone else could not retrieve it.

Jesus cleans up our lives.

Jesus cleans up our lives. This cleansing process is called sanctification.

Justification is the term, which describes God's gracious gift of forgiveness and right standing in his sight. It is a judicial term, which means I am pronounced, "Not guilty." It is "just as if I'd never sinned."

Our justification is not based on anything we do for ourselves. I do not achieve my justification. I receive my justification. I do not partner together with God for my justification. He saves me.

I was dead. *I was dead. DEAD.* I had no hope. I couldn't do a thing to save myself. When I was dead, he made me alive in Christ Jesus. *He saved me.*

The Galatians were told that they must not get circumcised, because they had bought into the idea that circumcision was something they could do to make themselves okay with God. The apostle Paul says, "No, absolutely not. It is essential that you understand that you have no hope except in Christ Jesus."

Once you know that Christ is your only hope, you have a solid basis for hope. If it's me and Jesus, I'm going to keep looking at the me part and thinking, I know Jesus is good, but I'm not sure about me. I've got problems.

Would you say the apostle Paul showed good evidence of knowing the Lord? Paul said:

I know whom I have believed, and am convinced that He is able to guard that which I have entrusted to him for that day.[39]

Three QUESTIONS

Paul had confidence of eternal life, because his confidence was in Jesus alone. Concerning this process of sanctification and getting to really know the Lord, Paul said of himself,

Not that I have already obtained all this, or have already been made perfect, but I press on to take hold of that for which Christ Jesus took hold of me.[40]

Our hope of eternal life is not based on our efforts. It's not based on our knowledge. It's based on God's grace alone. Once I understand this, then I can rest in his grace. I can have confidence, because my confidence is in him, not in me.

"When Satan tempts me to despair and tells me of the sin within," what do I do?

Where do you think you're going?

I look to Jesus, my Savior and my God. It's his righteousness I depend upon. He is my advocate.

"My faith has found a resting place, not in device or creed. I trust in his unchanging grace, his blood avails for me. I need no other confidence; I need no other plea. It is enough that Jesus died and that he died for me."[41]

This is why I know where I'm going. I know I'm going to heaven. Jesus said so. He always keeps his promises. He said,

Do not let your hearts be troubled. Trust in God; trust also in me. In my Father's house are many rooms; if it were not so, I would have told you. I am going there to prepare a place for you. And if I go and prepare a place

for you, I will come back and take you to be with me that you also may be where I am.[42]

Because I know I'm going to my Father's house, it changes everything about how I want to live here and now.

I'm going to the Father's house. I am part of God's family. He has redeemed me. He has adopted me. He has caused me to be born again to a living hope. My confidence is in him. Because I know I'm going to my Father's house, it changes everything about how I want to live here and now.

I want to make investments in eternity now, because this life is so short. Our life on earth is like a vapor. It's over so quickly.

Where do you think you're going?

Billy Graham has said several times in recent years that the biggest surprise of his life is how quickly it has gone by. Occasionally, some of us get a glimpse of this when we realize that our children are the age we think of ourselves as being. All of a sudden, I realize, "If my son is that age, I can't be that age anymore."

I regularly went to see my very elderly mom. She lived to be ninety-nine. At the end of her life she had senile dementia, but she still loved Jesus and she still loved me. We'd talk a little bit and then she'd say, "Well, you're looking well."

I routinely responded, "Thank you, Mom. Do you know how old I am now?"

Three QUESTIONS

"No, how old are you?"

Year after year, I would answer, "I'm fifty-three ... fifty-four ... fifty-five ... fifty-six."

She consistently asked with amazement, "Then, how old am I?"

When I told her, she said predictably, "No. Really?"

"Yes, ma'am."

"Am I really?"

"Yes, ma'am."

"Well, that's just hard to believe. God has been kind, hasn't he?"

"Yes, ma'am, he has."

Where do you think you're going?

My mom lived to be almost a hundred, but she's gone now. I will be soon. You will be soon. We're all going to spend eternity somewhere, and we need to live our days now in light of the fact that we're going to spend eternity somewhere.

If you have not come to know Jesus, I plead with you, give your life to him. Meditate on your identity in Christ. If you aren't in Christ, if you don't really know him, if Jesus is someone about whom you believe certain things but not someone you know on a personal level, I plead with you to trust him as your Savior and Lord. Ask him to save you. If you're not sure that you know him, tell him.

Three QUESTIONS

Say to him, "I'm not sure I really know you. I want to know you. Please, change my heart."

None of us deserves God's grace.

None of us deserves God's grace. None of us is worthy. None of us is good enough. No one who thinks they deserve God's grace is saved. We all need God's grace. This is what makes it grace.

And, if you already know you belong to Jesus, live like it.

What do you think you're doing?

When I was a child, I heard a story. I wish I had a copy of it, because I'm sure it was written in much more poetic fashion than I can recall it. Remember, I heard it as a child.

Three QUESTIONS

Two men were working on a construction site. Someone passing by asked the two men, "What are you doing?"

One of the men replied with agitation, "I'm digging a ditch."

The other man at the exact same construction site, digging the same ditch, responded, "I'm helping to build a cathedral."

Both answers were true, but one fellow could only see the ditch. That's what he focused on. The other fellow understood that what he was doing down there in the dirt had much bigger implications. He wasn't just digging a ditch. He was contributing to the construction of a magnificent edifice.

What do you think you're doing?

 What do you think you're doing?

This question of perspective impacts every area of our lives.

I had the privilege of growing up in the town of Montreat, North Carolina. When I lived there, we had one hundred-fifty year-round residents. I moved there at age twelve into my ninety-year-old grandmother's home. My dad was in a tough church situation as pastor, so he decided to opt for mental health and early retirement.

My grandmother and aunt turned their basement into living quarters for my father, mother and me. My aunt and mother worked, and my dad took care of his mother and the home.

Three QUESTIONS

Because Montreat was such a small town, we had the opportunity to get to know some wonderful neighbors quite well, among them Dr. and Mrs. Billy Graham. Again, we knew them not because we were special people but because there were one hundred-fifty year-round residents, and the Grahams were good neighbors. They lived right up the road from us.

Many folks from Ridgecrest, the Baptist conference center, used to stop by our house asking for directions to the Grahams. Very often, I would ask these folks, usually a preacher and spouse, sometimes a couple of preachers riding in the front seat and their spouses in the backseat, "Do you have an invitation to the Graham home?"

What do you think you're doing?

Simultaneously, one would say yes and the other would say no. They would look at each other, realizing that they should have gotten their story straight. I was glad there was one person in the car telling the truth. In any case, I would give the directions but explain to them, "If you go on up the street you'll come to the gate, and you can't go past that point."

On a number of occasions, I went inside the gate all the way up to the house and actually spent time there. Ruth had built a beautiful home out of antique logs she had harvested from old tobacco barns and other old buildings around the countryside. She had them brought to Montreat and constructed into a modest but very beautiful home. She raised her five children in this home, while Dr. Graham was continually on the road. Ruth filled the home with antiques and love.

Serving others is divine worship

Among the antiques was on old sign from an Anglican church that Ruth had picked up somewhere. As I recall, the sign said, "Divine service rendered here three times daily." She put that sign right over the kitchen sink. Ruth wanted to remind herself that when she was doing the dishes, she wasn't just doing the dishes. She was doing the dishes, caring for her family, as an act of worship. Serving others is divine worship, divine service.

What do you think you're doing?

Paul says in Romans 12:1:

Therefore, I urge you, brothers, in view of God's mercy, to offer your bodies as living sacrifices, holy and pleasing to God – this is your spiritual act of worship.

Offer your bodies as living sacrifices.

JB Philips paraphrases this passage accurately: "This is intelligent worship." This is right-minded. We worship God intelligently by yielding everything to him.

When we read the phrase, "offer your bodies," all of a sudden it gets practical, doesn't it?

Three QUESTIONS

Some of us would rather keep it cerebral. We want to sit in our seats and pray, "God, I am yours."

Then, God says, "Go, do this."

Our response is to pray, "Oh yes, God. I want you to know that I see the need. I will pray that something will get done." We say, "Here am I, Lord, send Aaron."

Right? We see the need. We know somebody ought to do something.

I can't count the number of times as a pastor people have come to me to say, "I think our church ought to fund this thing."

My question is, "How much are you putting in?"

What do you think you're doing?

The person sincerely believes the project needs funding, but what they mean is that the church, those other people, should give some of their money.

I'm great at this, too. I see the need and I think of the right person to pay for the project.

God says to me, "Look, the fields are white unto harvest. What are you going to do about it?"

Ask the Lord of the harvest, therefore, to send out workers into his harvest field.[43]

Do you remember this story? The very next thing that happens in the text is that Jesus sends forth the disciples. This is a pattern in Scripture and in life.

Three QUESTIONS

God speaks to our hearts, enlarges our vision and sensitizes us to the needs around us. We see the need and we say, "Oh God, this is a tremendous need. Please, do something."

God says, "I'm going to use you."

That's how I ended up doing what I now do. When I was a teenager, God broke my heart with the needs of children who come from shattered situations. As I wept and cried out to God and said, "God you have to do something," God spoke to my heart and said, "I will do something, but I want to use you."

I'm glad God doesn't ask us to carry all the water ourselves, but we can't stay distant and uninvolved. We have to offer our body as a living sacrifice. It gets physical. We have to get personally involved. We can't just think about it. We can't just pray about it. We have to do whatever God requires.

Obedience to Christ impacts how we approach everything we do.

Obedience to Christ impacts our approach to everything we do.

I love my wife. I thank God that I've been blessed with such a fabulous helpmeet. She truly is wonderful. I mean this from the bottom of my heart. However, there are days when I don't feel the love as enthusiastically as I do after a romantic weekend at Grove Park Inn.

Three QUESTIONS

You may wake up every day and think, "Oh thank God, it's a new day, another opportunity to serve God and love my spouse," but I don't always wake up that way in the morning.

What I have to realize is that on those occasions when love demands of me a behavior that doesn't just flow naturally from my flesh, I must love my wife as Christ loved the church as an act of worship to God. In other words, there are times when I'm nice to Susan because she is so loveable; but there are other times when I'm nice to Susan because Jesus says, "This is how you show your love for me."

What do you think you're doing?

Jesus says to us, *I tell you the truth, whatever you did for one of the least of these brothers of mine, you did for me.*[44]

If I want to worship God, to show love for God and gratitude to God, I have to find opportunities to give to folks who can't pay me back. To do things for people I wouldn't ordinarily be inclined to do things for. To serve folks who other people don't want to serve. To give in ways that won't garner recognition for me.

Jesus said in the Sermon on the Mount, "If you're just nice to people who are nice to you, what are you doing that's different from others? The pagans do that." Of course, we all know it's true.

Three QUESTIONS

What is our holiday gift exchange about? I would submit to you that there is something fundamentally wrong with feeling an obligation to give gifts to people when we can't think of anything they need or want. If you don't know what to get, don't get anything.

Give to somebody who could actually benefit, and give in honor of the person who already has everything. Why in the world would you want to give one more thing to someone who has to say, "Oh well, thank you. You really shouldn't have."

You know he really means it, too. You really shouldn't have. It's just stupid. We do this every year, many of us more than once a year. There are birthdays,

What do you think you're doing?

too. And, what are we going to do for their anniversary?

I have received so many stupid gifts over the years and felt obliged to hang onto them for a little while, just in case the giver asks. Eventually, we pass these things on to the local rescue mission or another charitable receiver like Salvation Army. Somebody needs to get the benefit out of the gift.

We waste so much time, energy and money when there are real needs of real people with real pain that we could address. We could do something for someone who can't pay us back. It's not a sin to give Christmas presents, but remember whose birthday it is, would you? Give your gifts to Jesus. You'll find his address when you find somebody who can't pay you back.

I'm not saying you can't give to your relatives. If you have relatives, like some of my relatives, they probably have needs and can't pay you back. Generally, these aren't the relatives I like to give to. I don't really enjoy giving to relatives who have made stupid decisions with their money as much as I enjoy giving to the nice ones who like to give to me.

What pleases Jesus?

It's fine to give party favors to all the guests, but remember whose birthday it is. What pleases Jesus?

What do you think you're doing?

The birthday gifts should go to the birthday boy. Make sure the focus of your celebration is the worship of God and that it's not monetary; most importantly, make the celebration involve the way you serve others.

 What do you think you're doing?

When working with the children at the Ranch, there are times when I wonder, "Why am I doing this? I don't think these kids appreciate me the way they should."

Have you ever unselfishly set out to do something for the glory of God? You are determined to do something for somebody who can't pay you back. Then, you get hurt and maybe even angry that the recipient doesn't seem as grateful as they should be. Has this ever happened to you?

It happens to me sometimes. Here I am knocking myself out in order to do something for somebody who clearly does not deserve it, but I'm doing this "as unto the Lord." That was the original theory, but somehow I become put off at this person's apparent lack of appreciation. I don't insist that they kiss my feet, but it would be nice if they would at least say, "Thank you, Sir."

Have you ever felt this way with your own children? Have you ever felt like you just finished cleaning and they come walking in without checking their feet? They don't notice that the floor is clean, and they leave tracks on it again. You might say to them, "Honey, I just cleaned that floor," and they respond, "Oh, sorry Mom. What's for dinner?"

In that moment you want to say, "Mop the floor, and we'll talk about it."

I'm doing this stuff for them for HIM.

Do you have thoughts like this? I do. I have to remind myself that I'm not doing this stuff for "them." I'm doing this stuff for "them" for HIM.

He's appreciative, although he doesn't need to be appreciative of me. The fact is I don't just owe him a lot; I owe him everything.

Three QUESTIONS

I've often heard people say, "I owe a lot to God."

You don't owe a lot to God; You owe everything to God. You and I can't draw our next breath apart from his grace. Everything we have, we owe to him. So, when we do something as an act of divine service, as our reasonable service, our intelligent worship, yielding our bodies to him to do what he says, it doesn't begin to repay the debt we owe. We owe him everything. As Paul says to the Corinthians, *What do you have that you did not receive?*[45]

When I was a college student, I worked as a janitor in the college library. When the library was built in honor of Billy Graham's father-in-law, I landed the job as the first janitor. I was the first janitor in the Dr. L. Nelson Bell library at Montreat College. Nobody else can say that.

I took my job very seriously, including getting down on my hands and knees and scrubbing all the heel marks off the white tile. People with soft rubber heels marked the floor with every step they took. When the library closed at night, I would clean so that when the library opened the next morning, the place looked brand new, shiny and clean. I thought, "I am a good janitor. I do this for the glory of God."

During the time I worked as a janitor, somebody asked me to sing at a wedding. I felt honored and delighted. I love to sing, especially worship songs. When I found out they planned to pay me for singing, I felt awkward. I had never been paid to sing. I thought, "That's not right. Singing is a gift. To get paid to sing is wrong." I think I must have felt it would be humble to refuse payment for a talent God had given to me.

God slapped me down real fast. He told me: "Jim, you need to be grateful you're getting paid to sing. You need to be grateful you're getting paid to scrub heel marks off the floor. Not only could you not sing if I hadn't given you the ability to sing, you couldn't scrub heel marks off the floor if I hadn't given you the physical stamina to do that day after day."

What do you think you're doing?

I had to adjust my attitude. This was a paradigm shift. I thought there were certain things, which God had given to me as gifts. I viewed anything else as the things I did for myself and by myself: "This is my world. Being a janitor may not be very impressive, but I am a good janitor. I work hard, and I earn my paycheck."

You need to be thankful for everything, and it all belongs to God.

God said to me, "Everything you do, everything you are, everything you have all comes from my hand. You need to thank me for everything you are and everything you have, and it all belongs to me - not just some of it. Not just the stuff you say you're giving back to me. It all belongs to me."

There are times when we aren't paid for the work we do. Does this mean such labor is not valuable? Of course not.

...[Our] labor in the Lord is not in vain.[46]

God can get his hands on your stuff anytime he wants. Whether you choose to give it or not, God can get his hands on it anytime.

I know some people who chose not to give it, and God decided to let the devil take it. Even the devil has to work for God. Read the book of Job. In fact read Genesis, Exodus, Leviticus, Numbers, Deuteronomy, Joshua, Judges, Ruth....

What do you think you're doing?

God runs the universe. His hands aren't tied, and everything belongs to him. When we give back to God a portion of that which he has given to us, we're not giving God something new. He is pleased to receive it. He has a purpose, and he blesses. He promises to bless. He blesses as we give. But never, ever lose sight of the fact that it's all his to start with. It's all his. This is why we give what we give, and this is why we can give generously. It's all his.

The money we designate for God is God's, and the money we keep for ourselves is God's as well. It also belongs to God. Everything belongs to God.

Three QUESTIONS

The earth is the Lord's, and everything in it.[47]

...for every animal of the forest is mine, and the cattle on a thousand hills.[48]

The cattle farmer may not know this scripture, but God does, and God's people should. He doesn't just own the cattle, by the way, the sheep are also his. The fish in the deep and the stars in the sky belong to God. He created everything and he is Lord of all.

So, ...

 What do you think you're doing?

What do you think you're doing?

In his letter to the Thessalonians the apostle Paul writes:

Make it your ambition to lead a quiet life, to mind your own business and to work with your hands, just as we told you, so that your daily life may win the respect of outsiders and so that you will not be dependent on anybody.[49]

Does that Scripture reflect what you want for your children or would you rather that your child be a star?

"I didn't make it as a celebrity, but my child can."

"Come on, honey, Daddy wants you to be a success."

Three QUESTIONS

Would you honestly say from the heart to your child, "Make it your ambition to live a quiet life and work with your hands?"

Would you honestly say from the heart to your child, "Make it your ambition to live a quiet life and work with your hands?"

"I was hoping my child wouldn't have to work with his hands. He has delicate hands. Maybe we can compromise; he'd be a good pianist."

I would submit to you that many of us grew up in a culture saturated with the wrong value system. We have placed a premium on a lot of stuff that handicaps our children, our ministries, and us,

We have placed a premium on a lot of stuff that handicaps our children.

because far too often we tend to value what the world values and not what God values. I cannot count the number of times I have gone to the Scriptures and been astounded by the fact that God's strategy is the opposite of what mine would be.

God wants to start a new nation, so he picks a childless couple and makes them wait until they are beyond any hope of having children, and then he gives Abraham and Sarah their son, Isaac. I wouldn't have done it like that. If I were trying to start a new nation, I would have picked a young, fertile couple.

Three QUESTIONS

Doesn't my strategy make more sense to you?

God wants to bring his people out of bondage, so he picks a guy with a speech impediment named Moses to be his spokesman. God waits to call him until he's eighty-years-old and has a criminal record. I wouldn't have done it that way. In fact, I would have advised God against the whole plan.

God wants a king who can lead his people in triumph over their enemies, so God picks a shepherd boy who seems so insignificant that when it was time to call all the sons to dine with the prophet, David wasn't invited. I wouldn't have picked David, but God said to Samuel, *Man looks at the outward appearance, but the LORD looks at the heart.*[50]

David was "a man after God's own heart."[51]

In the gospels, we read a cast of all the celebrities, all the big shots, all the powerful. Then, we read, ... *the word of God came to John... in the desert.*[52]

Why didn't God send his Word to one of the important people? These people were in positions of power and influence. If God had sent his Word to them, they could have done something about it. But God said, "No, John the Baptist is my chosen forerunner. He's going to introduce my son, Jesus."

Three QUESTIONS

God is able to use you in this life to accomplish things you would never ever have imagined.

I don't know who you think you are. I don't know where you think you're going. But, please understand, if you are a child of God on your way to the Father's house, God is able to use you in this life to accomplish things you would never, ever have imagined.

You may think, "I don't have the natural gifts for that."

Great. Perfect. Do you know what Paul said was one of his major qualifications to be the apostle that he was? Chief of sinners. How would you like that on your resume? Would we have picked Paul to be the writer of more of the New Testament than anybody else?

"So, Paul, tell us your background. How did you get this assignment?"

"Well, I used to persecute Christians, so I guess you could say I have exposure to Christianity. I used to round them up and have them beaten and tortured to death."

I would have said, "God, please excuse me. I need to give you some background on this guy. He's the wrong choice, a bad fellow, not to be trusted."

God says, "I know all about him."

"No, no, no, no, no. You don't. He's a bad man, a really bad man."

"I know. I know. Here's what I'm going to do. I'm going to give him a new heart. I will put my Spirit within him. He's going to shine for me. He will suffer greatly, but he will be my spokesman."

God calls his people to do things they can only do supernaturally. Not everyone has a national or international ministry, but you can't even be the kind of husband or the kind of wife God is calling you to be apart from his supernatural power.

Marriage isn't just about you finding somebody to be your companion. Marriage is about your opportunity to witness to all who know you, as you exemplify the relationship between Christ and the church.

For this reason a man will leave his father and mother and be united to his wife, and the two will become one flesh. This is a profound mystery—but I am talking about Christ and the church. However, each one of you also must love his wife as he loves himself, and the wife must respect her husband.[53]

You cannot be the kind of parent God is calling you to be apart from the supernatural power of God's Holy Spirit at work in you. You are supposed to show your children what God's love, truth, holiness, and patience look like. You can't do this apart from God's Holy Spirit at work in you.

Three QUESTIONS

You cannot be the kind of employer, employee or co-worker God has called you to be apart from the supernatural power of the Holy Spirit.

You cannot be the kind of citizen or neighbor God has called you to be apart from the supernatural power of the Holy Spirit.

 What do you think you're doing?

Everything we do, as followers of Jesus Christ, is for the glory of God.

So whether you eat or drink or whatever you do, do it all for the glory of God.[54]

I don't always live up to this. Recently, I made an ice cream sundae for myself at a gathering of fellow Christians. I didn't properly assess the volume capacity of the glass dish. There were other glass dishes, but I wanted to get all the ice cream I wanted into one glass dish. Then, I added chocolate sauce on top of the bananas I had put on it. I wasn't walking in the Spirit as I made my sundae; I was walking in the flesh.

I apologized to the people who may have seen the grotesque sight of me licking the outside of my ice cream dish. It is embarrassing to be a pig. I realize that people hear what I say as a preacher and think I must be pretty spiritual. Then, they see me with a dish of ice cream and become confused. I don't want to be considered phony, but I assure you I need to die daily to my selfish, foolish sin nature.

Three QUESTIONS

My wife wasn't there as I served myself ice cream. I like having my wife with me. She keeps me in line in these situations. Susan would have said, "Don't put so much in your bowl. You can have some of mine." She wasn't there and I wanted it all for me.

Whatever you do, do it all for the glory of God.[55]

Offer your bodies as living sacrifices, holy and pleasing to God — this is your spiritual act of worship.[56]

We need each other for accountability.

We need each other for accountability, and we need to realize that the Spirit-filled life isn't automatic. The details do matter and we need

136

to progress in our walk.

How marvelous that God calls us to represent him in a world filled with need. We are called to serve people who can't pay us back. They don't have to, because everything we have came from God anyway. Everything we are belongs to him. This is a privilege, and we find our joy in meeting Jesus in "the least of these."[57]

So, ...

Christian, *who do you think you are?*

Your identity is in Christ! Take time to study the Scriptures and begin to believe what God says about your real identity. He sees his children in the context of the righteousness of Christ.

137

Three QUESTIONS

He is our righteousness and our peace. He is our sufficiency. Dearly loved child of God, learn to rest in the Father's embrace, and be grateful that your identity is not your achievement. It is his gift of grace.

Where do you think you're going? Your destiny is with Christ in glory! Jesus is preparing a place for us even now. There will be no more sickness or suffering or pain. We will never be lonely or confused or fearful again. He will wipe away every tear from our eyes. The beauty and the joy of that place will exceed even our capacity to imagine.

What do you think you're doing?
Your calling is to serve Christ in preparation for the day when we will gather at his throne. Therefore, everything you do now is eternally significant.

You may wonder why some things happen and some prayers seem to go unanswered. You may suffer repeated crushing disappointments and discouragement that test your faith, but if you will continue in obedience, you will see in eternity that all of God's promises are true.

Our greatest point of blessing is often tied to our greatest pain. God is not cruel but his power is manifest most clearly in our weakness.[58]

139

Three QUESTIONS

Don't be afraid!

Don't be afraid! When the night is long and the wind blows hard against you, remember who you are. Remember where you are going. And, remember what you are doing.

Endnotes

[1] John 8:44.

[2] James 2:19.

[3] Romans 14:11.

[4] 2 Peter 1:10.

[5] Matthew 7:22, 23.

[6] I Corinthians 6:9-11.

[7] 1 John 5:2,3a.

[8] 1 John 4:20.

[9] 1 John 5:13.

[10] 1 John 1:9.

[11] Galatians 5:4.

[12] Galatians 5.

[13] John 3:36 Scripture quotation taken from the New American Standard Bible®,

[14] 1 Peter 2:9.

[15] 1 Peter 2:11,12.

[16] John 12:25.

[17] 1 John 2:15.

[18] John 15:9.

[19] Romans 12:2.

[20] Romans 12:2.

[21] 1 Peter 2:9.

[22] John 15:5.

[23] Psalm 100:3b.

[24] Matthew 5:13, 14.

[25] Romans 12:1,2.

[26] 1 Corinthians 15:19.

27 Hebrews 9:27.
28 William Doane and Robert Lowry (New York: Bigelow & Main, 1876)

29 Luke 23:43.

30 Matthew 7:22, 23.

31 Matthew 7:23.

32 Romans 3:23; 6:23.

33 Numbers 22:28.

34 Hebrews 12:2.

35 Romans 2:4.

36 Titus 3:3-7.

37 Luke 10:21.

38 Mark 10:15.

39 Timothy 1:12.

40 Philippians 3:12.
41 Words: Eliza Hewitt, 1891. Music: Andre Gretry (1741-1813).

[42] John 14:1-3.

[43] Luke 10:2.

[44] Matthew 25:40.

[45] 1 Corinthians 4:7.

[46] 1 Corinthians15:58.

[47] Psalm 24:1.

[48] Psalm 50:10.

[49] 1 Thessalonians 4:11.

[50] 1 Samuel 16:7.

[51] Acts 13:22.

[52] Luke 3:2.

[53] Ephesians 5:31-33.

[54] 1 Corinthians 10:31.

[55] 1 Corinthians 10:31.

[56] Romans 12:2.

[57] Matthew 25:40.

2 Corinthians 12:1-10.

Visit us @WVR.org

Listen to Jim on *Abiding in Christ*

- Weekdays on **SiriusXM** 131
- Download programs at WVR.org
- Jim's audio and video content is also available on Sermonaudio.com

View sermons and devotionals at WVR.org